Divine Dining

FOODS FROM THE BIBLE

AWARD-WINNING NEW YORK CHEF
Lance Nitahara
&
BEST-SELLING AUTHOR
Ray Comfort

BRIDGE LOGOS

Newberry, FL 32669

Divine Dining: Foods from the Bible
By Lance Nitahara and Ray Comfort

Bridge-Logos, Inc.
Newberry, FL 32669, USA

Edited by Lynn Copeland

Recipe photographs: Natasha M. Harris

Cover photograph: Photography by Aubrey Rae

Addtional photographs from iStock Photos (pp. 11, 15, 25) and 123rf (pp. 6, 17, 55, 59, 64)

Cover, page design, and production by Genesis Group

ISBN 978-1-61036-274-0

Library of Congress Control Number: 2022937688

Printed in the United States of America

Pictured on the front cover: Broiled Tilapia Amandine (page 18), Grilled Veal Chops (page 8), and Bread Pudding with Figs (page 65).

*To Kelli, my wife, best friend, and partner in ministry,
who has grown more of the fruit of patience for me than
anyone I have ever known. The Lord has blessed me in
many ways, but none like the day that I found you.*
~Lance

Contents

Entrees

Sides & Sweets

The Hawaiian Table

Introduction

Ray and I set out to offer a cookbook that presented a varied, vibrant assortment of recipes from around the world that had one thing in common: the use of ingredients that were mentioned within the pages of the greatest book ever written, the Holy Bible. While a few of the dishes found in this book might have been found gracing the table of someone in the geographical and biblical era of the Lord Jesus, most of them are quite modern and many of them will likely be very familiar too! While writing the recipes for this book, I learned so much about how food was an integral part of Scripture, as well as the supporting roles it played in telling the story that points to our blessed Savior. Please enjoy cooking these dishes as much as we enjoyed putting them together into this culinary collection for you.

In the last section, called "The Hawaiian Table," I am delighted to include a few delicacies from Hawaii that were quite standard fare when I was growing up there. Ray suggested that I include them to give readers a bit of a personal taste of my childhood. I hope you enjoy these recipes that might be found at a luau, a family get-together, or simply on the everyday Hawaiian dinner table. Note: Some of the recipes have been modified to allow for ingredients that may not be readily available outside of the Aloha state.

We hope you enjoy this book.

May God bless you and keep you,

Lance Nitahara & Ray Comfort

The Most Important Food

Eating not only keeps us alive, but it is one of this life's greatest pleasures. However, Jesus spoke of a special food that is far more important than physical food. He said,

> "Do not labor for the food which perishes, but for the food which endures to everlasting life, which the Son of Man will give you, because God the Father has set His seal on Him." (John 6:27)

To eat a lifetime of delicious food and then miss out on the food of which Jesus spoke is to strain at the gnat and swallow the camel. Therefore, let's take a moment to look at the food which endures to everlasting life.

Do you know what death is, according to the Bible? It's wages. Scripture says, "The wages of sin is death" (Romans 6:23). Sin is so serious to God that He gives sinners the death sentence. It's like a judge in a court of law who sentences a criminal to death for raping and viciously murdering three young girls. The criminal has earned the electric chair. This is what he deserves; it's his wages. Let's see what wages you will earn.

Do you think you are a good person? No doubt, like most of us, you do. How many lies do you think you have told in your life? Have you ever stolen something, even if it's small? If you've done these two things, then you are a lying thief. Have you ever used God's name in vain, either flippantly (including "OMG") or as profanity? If you have, let me ask you if you would ever use your mother's name as a cuss word. I'm sure you wouldn't, because that would show you don't respect her in the slightest. And yet you have used God's holy name as a cuss word. That's called "blasphemy," and it's very serious in God's eyes. He promises that whoever takes His name in vain will not be guiltless. One more question. Jesus said that if we look with lust we commit adultery in our heart. Have you ever looked at someone with lust? If you're normal, you have.

So here is a summation of your court case. If you're like most of us, you have admitted to being a lying, thieving, blasphemous adulterer at heart. So on Judgment Day, when God judges you by the Ten Commandments, are you going to be innocent or guilty? Guilty, of course. Will you therefore go to Heaven or Hell? The answer is that if you die in your sins, you have God's promise that you will end up in Hell. The wages you've earned is the death sentence. The Bible says that all liars will be cast into the lake of fire, and no thief, no adulterer, and no blasphemer will inherit the kingdom of God.

The Ten Commandments, a few of which we've just looked at, are God's "moral Law." You and I broke the Law, but Jesus paid the fine in His life's blood. That's what happened when He died on the cross. That's why He said just before He died, "It is finished!" In other words, the debt has been paid in full. If you're in court and someone pays your fine, the judge can let you go even though you are guilty. In doing so, he still does what is legal, right, and just. Does that make sense? Even though you are guilty, you are free to walk out of the courtroom, because someone has paid your fine.

The Bible says, "God demonstrates His own love toward us, in that while we were still sinners, Christ died for us" (Romans 5:8). God proved His great love for you through the cross. Then Jesus rose from the dead and defeated the power of the grave.

It is because Jesus paid the fine for sin on the cross that God can dismiss your case. You can walk out of His courtroom on Judgment Day. He can commute your death sentence and legally let you live forever, all because Jesus paid the fine for sin in full on that cross. Does that make sense? He paid the fine, so you can be free from the penalty of death. God has made the way to find everlasting life so simple that a child can understand it. All you need to do is be honest and humble. You simply have to repent of your sins and trust in Jesus alone. Repentance means to turn from sin. You can't say you're a Christian and continue to lie, steal, and blaspheme God's name. That would be to deceive yourself and play the hypocrite. Your repentance must be sincere to be genuine. Then you trust in Jesus alone, as you would trust in a parachute. You do what the Bible says to do—"put on the Lord Jesus Christ" (Romans 13:14).

So today, repent and trust in Jesus, because the reality is, you may not have tomorrow. If you're not sure how to repent, here is a model prayer of repentance, given to us in Scripture when King David had his sin exposed:

> Have mercy upon me, O God, according to Your lovingkindness; according to the multitude of Your tender mercies, blot out my transgressions. Wash me thoroughly from my iniquity, and cleanse me from my sin. For I acknowledge my transgressions, and my sin is always before me. Against You, You only, have I sinned, and done this evil in Your sight—that You may be found just when You speak, and blameless when You judge. (Psalm 51:1–4)

Whatever you do, don't trust in your goodness to save you, as most people do. That's like flapping your arms when you jump out of a plane. It's not going to work. You're not a good person; you're like the rest of us. Transfer your trust from yourself to the Savior. We trust doctors and pharmaceutical companies when we take pills, cables when we step into an elevator, and pilots when we fly on planes. Doctors can make mistakes, elevators can let us down, and pilots sometimes make deadly errors. But God will never let you down. He is without sin, and because of that, the Scriptures tell us that it is impossible for Him to lie. Therefore, trust Him with all of your heart, right now. Please, don't put it off for another second. Then make sure you pick up a Bible and read it daily, and obey what you read. Prayer is us talking to God, but reading the Bible is God speaking to us, and we need to be swift to hear and slow to speak.

As much as we hope you enjoy these recipes for physical food, our prayer is that most importantly you will feast on Jesus, who the Bible calls the "bread of life." He is the food which endures to everlasting life.

> "I am the living bread which came down from heaven.
> If anyone eats of this bread, he will live forever."
> (John 6:51)

Abbreviations used:

c.	*cup*
tsp.	*teaspoon*
T.	*tablespoon*
oz.	*ounce*
lb.	*pound*

Entrees

Roasted Quail
Stuffed with Farro and Figs

Yield: 4 servings

Ingredients:

Farro Stuffing

3 tsp. olive oil, divided
1 clove garlic, minced
¼ c. leeks, sliced thin
1 c. pearled farro
2 c. water
kosher salt and pepper to taste
4 dried figs, chopped

Roast Quail

4 semi-boneless quail
1 T. olive oil
kosher salt and pepper to taste
2 tsp. fresh rosemary leaves, chopped
1 tsp. fresh thyme leaves
4 cloves garlic, crushed
1 c. chicken broth or stock
2 tsp. white wine vinegar
1 oz. butter, diced

Instructions:

1. In a small saucepan, heat 2 tsp. olive oil over medium heat until shimmering. Add garlic and leeks and cook until softened but not browned.

2. Add farro and toast in oil for 1 minute.

3. Add water and bring to a boil. Boil the farro, stirring occasionally, until tender to the bite, about 20–25 minutes.

4. Drain water from the farro and stir in remaining 1 tsp. olive oil and season with salt and pepper. Fold in chopped figs. Cool farro and reserve.

5. Preheat oven to 350 degrees F.

6. Rub quail with olive oil and season with salt and pepper. Stuff the cavity of the quail with rosemary, thyme, and crushed garlic cloves (1 per bird).

7. Heat a large sauté pan over medium-high heat. Brown quail on all sides until golden brown. Remove pan from heat, and stuff quail with cooked farro mixture.

8. Return stuffed quail to sauté pan and place into oven and roast until the internal temperature of quail reaches 165 degrees F, about 5–6 minutes.

9. Remove quail from pan and keep warm.

10. Place pan with drippings over medium heat on stovetop. Add chicken broth and deglaze drippings from bottom of pan. Continue simmering to reduce stock by half.

11. Add white wine vinegar and simmer for 1 more minute.

12. Remove pan from heat and add butter. With a whisk, swirl butter until completely melted and emulsified into sauce. Season with salt and pepper.

13. Serve quail warm with sauce.

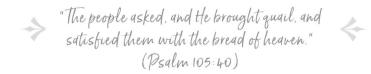

"The people asked, and He brought quail, and
satisfied them with the bread of heaven."
(Psalm 105:40)

Squab (Pigeon) Tagine
with Olives and Lemon

Yield: 4 servings

Ingredients:

4 whole squab
4 T. olive oil
1 yellow onion, diced
2 carrots, peeled and sliced
2 cloves garlic, minced
2 tsp. ground cinnamon
2 tsp. ground coriander

1 tsp. mustard seeds
1 tsp. ground ginger
2 lemons, zested
2 c. chicken broth
1 c. green picholine olives
3 sprigs parsley, chopped fine
kosher salt and pepper to taste

Instructions:

1. Preheat oven to 350 degrees F.

2. Cut squab into 4 pieces, breasts and legs. Season all over with salt and pepper.

3. In a large saucepan or a rondeau, heat olive oil on stovetop until hot.

4. Place squab pieces into pan and sear on all sides until golden brown.

5. Remove squab from pan and add onion and carrots. Cook until lightly brown.

6. Add garlic to pan and cook until tender.

7. Add cinnamon, coriander, mustard seeds, and ginger and cook in oil until fragrant, about 1 minute.

8. Add lemon zest and chicken broth to pan. Return squab to pan. Cover and cook in oven for about 20–30 minutes, or until squab is tender.

9. Stir in olives and cook for 2 more minutes on stovetop. Finish with parsley and season to taste with salt and pepper.

Roast Partridge
with Caramelized Apple & Barley Salad

Yield: 4 servings

Ingredients:

Partridges

2 whole partridges
kosher salt and pepper to taste
4 sprigs fresh sage
4 sprigs fresh parsley
2 sprigs fresh thyme
3 T. vegetable oil
4 T. unsalted butter, softened

Apple and Barley Salad

2 c. pearled barley
1 T. vegetable oil
2 T. pine nuts
2 Granny Smith apples, diced
1 T. brown sugar
2 T. unsalted butter
2 T. white wine vinegar
3 T. olive oil
kosher salt and pepper to taste

Sauce

¼ c. apple cider
1 c. chicken broth or stock
1 tsp. butter (salted)

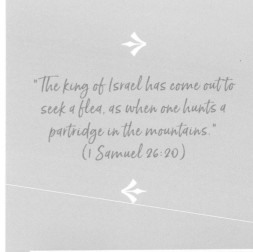

"The king of Israel has come out to seek a flea, as when one hunts a partridge in the mountains."
(1 Samuel 26:20)

Instructions:

1. Preheat oven to 400 degrees F.

2. Season partridges all over and inside with salt and pepper.

3. Remove leaves from sage, parsley, and thyme. Place stems inside the cavity of the partridges.

4. In a large sauté pan, heat 3 T. vegetable oil over medium-high heat until hot. Place partridges in pan, breast side down, and sear until golden brown. Turn partridges and repeat on other breast. Repeat on outside of thighs.

5. Lay partridges in pan, breast side up, and spread butter on top of breasts. Put pan in oven and roast until the center of breasts register 150 degrees F, approximately 20–30 minutes.

6. While partridges are cooking, in a medium saucepan, bring 1 quart of water to a boil. Add a generous pinch of salt. Add pearled barley and reduce to a simmer. Cook until barley is tender, about 20–25 minutes. Set aside.

7. In a large saucepan, add 1 T. vegetable oil. Heat over medium-high heat until hot. Add pine nuts to pan and stir until a light golden brown color has been achieved. Remove pine nuts from the pan with a slotted spoon.

8. While pan is hot, add apples and caramelize on top and bottom of each dice. Add brown sugar and 2 T. butter to pan and stir until brown sugar has melted.

9. Cover pan with aluminum foil and place into oven for about 5 minutes or until apples are tender and golden brown.

10. Place the cooked apples, barley, and pine nuts in a large mixing bowl. Add vinegar and olive oil. Season to taste with salt and pepper and toss to combine.

11. Once partridges are done, remove them from the oven and allow to rest for about 5 minutes. Using a sharp knife, remove legs and breasts from the bone.

12. Pour off excess fat from the pan and deglaze the pan with apple cider. Place pan on medium heat on the stovetop and simmer cider until reduced halfway. Then add chicken stock and reduce halfway. Finally, remove pan from heat and swirl in butter until fully melted and combined. Season to taste with salt and pepper and serve with roasted partridge legs and breasts.

Grilled Veal Chops
with Pomegranate Glaze

Yield: 4 servings

Ingredients:

4 bone-in veal chops, about 1-inch thick (approx. 2 lbs.)
2 T. olive oil
kosher salt and black pepper to taste
4 sprigs fresh thyme, chopped
2 sprigs fresh rosemary, chopped
3 oz. pomegranate molasses
2 oz. honey

Instructions:

1. Preheat a gas or charcoal grill to high heat (about 450 degrees F).

2. Using a pastry brush, brush veal with olive oil and coat with salt, pepper, and the chopped leaves of the thyme and rosemary.

3. Combine pomegranate molasses and honey in a separate bowl.

4. Place veal chops on the hottest part of the grill and cook both sides until deep, dark grill marks are achieved but meat is underdone in the center, about 2 minutes per side.

5. Move chops to a cooler area of the grill to continue cooking. As chops are cooking, brush glaze onto chops. Repeat glaze every 2–3 minutes until chops are cooked to desired doneness.

6. Allow chops to rest 2–3 minutes in a warm place. Serve with your favorite sides.

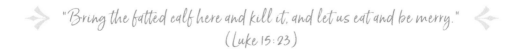

"Bring the fatted calf here and kill it, and let us eat and be merry."
(Luke 15:23)

Braised Oxtail
with Squash and Leeks

Yield: 4 servings

Ingredients:

3 lbs. beef oxtail
3 T. all-purpose flour
3 T. vegetable oil
4 oz. onions, diced
8 oz. leeks, white parts only, sliced thin
1 T. tomato paste
1 lb. butternut squash, peeled and diced
1 quart beef broth
kosher salt and pepper to taste

Instructions:

1. Preheat oven to 350 degrees F.

2. Season oxtail with salt and pepper. Toss with flour.

3. In a large, wide pot or Dutch oven, add vegetable oil and heat over medium heat until hot.

4. Sear oxtail in hot oil, browning on all sides.

5. Remove oxtail from pan. Add onions and cook until tender, about 2 minutes.

6. Add leeks. Cook until tender, about 2 minutes.

7. Add tomato paste and cook until the color of paste darkens and it begins to smell sweet.

8. Add butternut squash and toss until hot. Place oxtail back into pan, and add broth to come ¾ of the way up the oxtail.

9. Cover pot with lid and place into oven. Cook until oxtail is meltingly soft and falling off the bone, about 2–3 hours. Season well to taste and serve hot with butternut squash and leeks from the braising pan.

"So Elisha turned back from him, and took a yoke of oxen and slaughtered them and boiled their flesh, using the oxen's equipment, and gave it to the people, and they ate."
(1 Kings 19:21)

Beef en Croute

Yield: 4 servings

Ingredients:

Mushroom and Olive Duxelles

1 lb. mushrooms, white or cremini
¾ c. Kalamata olives, drained and rinsed
2 T. vegetable oil
1 shallot, finely chopped
2 cloves garlic, finely chopped
2 sprigs fresh thyme, leaves only
kosher salt and black pepper to taste

Tenderloin

2 lbs. beef tenderloin, trimmed
kosher salt and black pepper to taste
4 T. vegetable oil
flour, for dusting
1 sheet puff pastry, thawed
2 T. Dijon mustard
1 egg yolk
2 T. heavy whipping cream

Cream Sauce

1 T. shallots, finely minced
1 T. all-purpose flour
1 c. beef broth
½ c. heavy whipping cream
1 tsp. Dijon mustard
kosher salt and black pepper to taste

"The eyes of all look
expectantly to You,
And You give them their
food in due season."
(Psalm 145:15)

Instructions:

1. Chop mushrooms and olives very finely. Reserve.

2. In a medium sauté pan, add 2 T. vegetable oil and heat over high heat until shimmering. Add mushrooms and olives and sauté until slightly brown, stirring often.

3. Reduce heat to medium and add chopped shallot and garlic. Cook until softened.

4. Add thyme leaves and season to taste. Remove duxelles from pan and transfer to a wide container to cool.

5. Season tenderloin with salt and pepper.

6. Heat 4 T. vegetable oil in a large sauté pan and sear tenderloin on all sides until well browned. Remove tenderloin from pan to cool slightly and set pan aside to use for sauce.

7. Dust a cutting board or clean work surface with flour. Spread out puff pastry horizontally and roll it out using a rolling pin until it is about ¼-inch to ⅛-inch thick. It should be a rectangle at least 1 inch longer than the beef.

8. Preheat oven to 425 degrees F.

9. Starting at the bottom edge, spread cooled duxelles in an even layer over ¾ of the puff pastry, stopping 2 inches from the top. Place seared beef on top of the duxelles.

10. Using a pastry brush, brush a light coating of Dijon mustard over the beef.

11. Roll beef up in puff pastry stopping halfway to tuck in ends of pastry, as you would a burrito. Once beef is rolled up completely, place onto a parchment-lined baking sheet seam-side down.

12. Beat together egg yolk and heavy cream to make an egg wash. Brush a thin coating of egg wash over top and sides of pastry, taking care not to let too much drip down.

13. Using a paring knife, cut 2 or 3 small slits in the top of the pastry to enable venting while the beef roasts.

14. Bake in oven for 20–25 minutes until pastry is golden brown and center of beef registers 130 degrees on an instant-read thermometer.

15. To make the sauce, heat the pan used to sear the beef over medium heat on stovetop.

16. Add shallots and cook until softened.

17. Sprinkle flour into pan and cook for about 2 minutes, stirring often. Deglaze pan with beef broth, scraping pan to release browned bits. Add heavy whipping cream and bring to a simmer. Simmer until sauce is slightly thickened. Finish by stirring in Dijon mustard and seasoning to taste with salt and pepper.

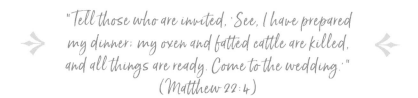

"Tell those who are invited, 'See, I have prepared my dinner; my oxen and fatted cattle are killed, and all things are ready. Come to the wedding.'"
(Matthew 22:4)

"It is good and fitting for one to eat and drink, and to enjoy the good of all his labor in which he toils under the sun all the days of his life which God gives him; for it is his heritage."
(Ecclesiastes 5:18)

Grilled Whole Snapper
Stuffed with Leeks, Lemon, and Peppers

Yield: 4 servings

Ingredients:

1 whole snapper (about 3 lbs.), scaled
kosher salt and black pepper to taste
2 T. olive oil
8 oz. leeks, sliced thin
½ lemon, sliced
6 oz. sweet peppers, sliced
1 tsp. fresh dill, chopped
2 tsp. fresh parsley, chopped

Instructions:

1. Soak a bamboo skewer in water.

2. Preheat a gas or charcoal grill to high.

3. Season cavity of snapper with salt and pepper.

4. Stuff cavity of snapper with leeks, lemon slices, and peppers. Secure cavity with the bamboo skewer.

5. Using a sharp knife, score the skin of the fish by making three cuts on each side. (This will help the skin not contract when grilling.) Rub 1 T. olive oil on the fish and season all over with salt and pepper.

6. Place fish on the hot grill. Once fish is cooked well and slightly charred on one side, flip it over and continue to cook the other side until an instant read thermometer reads an internal temperature of 135 degrees F. This should take about 6–8 minutes on each side.

7. Remove fish from grill, gently slide skewer out, and place fish on platter.

8. Drizzle more olive oil over top and garnish with dill and parsley.

9. Recommended: Serve with a side of couscous.

"We remember the fish which we ate freely
in Egypt, the cucumbers, the melons, the
leeks, the onions, and the garlic."
(Numbers 11:5)

Broiled Tilapia Amandine

Tilapia with Ezekiel's Grain Salad (recipe page 50)

Yield: 6 servings

Ingredients:

6 tilapia fillets
2 T. Dijon mustard
kosher salt and black pepper to taste
1 c. bread crumbs
4 oz. butter
½ c. sliced almonds
½ fresh lemon
1 T. fresh parsley, minced finely
kosher salt and black pepper to taste

Tilapia is probably the oldest farm-raised fish in the world. Stories from biblical scholars suggest it was the fish used by Jesus to feed the crowds at the Sea of Galilee. Today, over 80 nations produce farm-raised tilapia including the United States.

Instructions:

1. Preheat broiler in oven to low (400 degrees F).

2. Lay fillets on a cookie sheet or sheet pan that has been sprayed with pan coating.

3. Brush fillets with Dijon mustard and season with salt and pepper. Sprinkle bread crumbs over top to coat completely.

4. Melt butter and drizzle some over the crumbs on top of the fillets.

5. Place fillets under the broiler and broil until fish is golden brown on top and cooked through.

6. In a small pan, add melted butter and place over medium heat. Once butter has begun to brown slightly, add almonds and allow to toast while butter browns further.

7. When almonds are sufficiently toasted, remove pan from heat and squeeze lemon into butter.

8. Allow butter to cool slightly, add parsley, and season to taste.

9. Spoon the butter sauce over fish and serve with *Ezekiel's Grain Salad* (pictured).

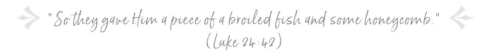

"So they gave Him a piece of a broiled fish and some honeycomb."
(Luke 24:42)

Tuna Carpaccio
with Cucumbers, Melon, Pickled Onions, and Crispy Leeks

Yield: 4 servings

Ingredients:

Carpaccio

6 oz. raw tuna, sushi-grade
1 jalapeno pepper
2 oz. cantaloupe, diced small
2 oz. cucumbers, peeled, seeded, sliced thin
1 T. olive oil
1 lemon
kosher salt and black pepper to taste

Pickled Onions

1 red onion, sliced thin
½ c. apple cider vinegar
2 tsp. sugar
1 tsp. kosher salt
½ c. hot water

Crispy Leeks

2 c. vegetable oil
2 oz. leeks, white part only, sliced thin
1 oz. all-purpose flour
kosher salt and black pepper to taste

Instructions:

1. For the pickled onions, combine vinegar, sugar, salt, and water in a pot and bring to a boil.

2. Put sliced onions in a bowl and pour hot pickling liquid over onions. Cover and allow to cool to room temperature. Reserve in refrigerator overnight.

3. For the crispy leeks, heat oil in a small saucepot to 325 degrees F.

4. Toss sliced leeks with salt, pepper, and flour in a bowl.

5. Fry floured leeks in oil until golden brown. Re-season and reserve in a warm place.

6. For the carpaccio, cover tuna with plastic wrap and place into freezer for about 1 hour until firm but not frozen solid. Using a very sharp knife, slice tuna into very thin slices and lay onto serving plates.

7. Cut jalapeno into paper-thin slices and lay over tuna.

8. Scatter cantaloupe over tuna.

9. Scatter sliced cucumber over tuna.

10. Drizzle olive oil over tuna. Using a citrus zester, zest lemon over tuna. Season with salt and pepper.

11. Top tuna with pickled onions and crispy fried leeks. Serve cold.

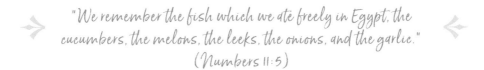

"We remember the fish which we ate freely in Egypt, the cucumbers, the melons, the leeks, the onions, and the garlic."
(Numbers 11:5)

Shakshuka
with Halloumi Cheese

*Originally hailing from Northern Africa, **Shakshuka** is an iconic one-pot Israeli breakfast dish, often served with pita bread or a hefty slice of challah. **Halloumi** is a Mediterranean cheese that does not easily melt, allowing it to be either fried or grilled before serving.*

Yield: 4 servings

Ingredients:

2 T. olive oil
1 medium yellow onion, sliced
2 red bell peppers, sliced
6 oz. hard chorizo sausage, diced small
1 tsp. smoked paprika
½ tsp. ground cumin
½ tsp. ground cinnamon
1 tsp. ground black pepper
2 tsp. kosher salt
12 oz. canned diced tomatoes
¼ c. water
6 large eggs
8 oz. halloumi cheese, diced small *(can substitute feta or fresh cheese curds)*
1 bunch cilantro leaves, roughly chopped
Crusty bread or matzo crackers to serve *(optional)*

Instructions:

1. Preheat oven to 400 degrees F.

2. Heat oil in a deep sauté pan or Dutch oven. When hot, add onion and cook over medium heat until tender and translucent.

3. Add peppers and cook for about 3 minutes more, until peppers have softened.

4. Add chorizo and cook for about a minute. Add spices, salt, and pepper. Cook for 1 more minute.

5. Add tomatoes to pan along with water. Stir into the rest of the ingredients and simmer on medium heat for about 10 minutes.

6. Make 6 small wells in the mixture and crack an egg into each.

7. Sprinkle diced halloumi on top of shakshuka and place pan into oven. Roast until the egg whites have set and the halloumi cheese has browned slightly.

8. Garnish with chopped cilantro and serve hot.

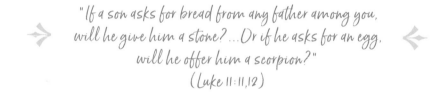

"If a son asks for bread from any father among you, will he give him a stone? ...Or if he asks for an egg, will he offer him a scorpion?"
(Luke 11:11,12)

"Listen, listen to me, and eat what is good,
and you will delight in the richest of fare."
(Isaiah 55:2)

Pistachio-Crusted Rack of Lamb

Yield: 4 servings

Ingredients:

3 lbs. racks of lamb, frenched
kosher salt and pepper to taste
3 T. vegetable oil
2 T. Dijon mustard
1 T. garlic, minced
4 oz. pistachios, shelled, unsalted
1 oz. panko bread crumbs
2 T. unsalted butter, melted

Instructions:

1. Preheat oven to 375 degrees F.

2. Season lamb all over with salt and pepper.

3. In a large sauté pan, add vegetable oil and heat over medium heat until hot. Sear lamb racks in hot oil, browning all sides.

4. Remove lamb from pan. Using a pastry brush, paint mustard all over lamb meat, avoiding getting any on the bones. Allow to rest for 5 minutes.

5. In the meantime, combine garlic, pistachios, and bread crumbs in a food processor. Pulse mixture until pistachios are coarsely chopped.

6. Pat nut and crumb mixture onto the lamb where mustard was painted on.

7. Season with more salt and pepper, then place lamb onto a sheet pan or cookie sheet.

8. Roast lamb racks in oven until internal temperature reaches 128 degrees F, about 10–15 minutes. Allow to rest for 5 minutes at room temperature before carving and serving.

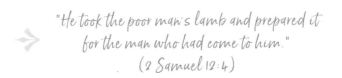

"He took the poor man's lamb and prepared it
for the man who had come to him."
(2 Samuel 12:4)

Lamb, Sweet Potato, and Feta Frittata

Yield: 4 servings

Ingredients:

1 lb. leg of lamb, boneless
1 T. kosher salt
1 tsp. black pepper
2 tsp. smoked paprika
2 T. + 2 tsp. olive oil
1 lemon, juiced
1 lb. sweet potatoes, peeled and diced
kosher salt and pepper to taste
4 oz. fresh spinach
8 large eggs
2 tsp. + 4 tsp. Italian parsley, chopped
1 c. + 2 T. feta cheese, crumbled
1 c. Greek yogurt

Instructions:

1. Preheat oven to 350 degrees F.

2. Combine salt, pepper, smoked paprika, 1 T. olive oil, and the juice of 1 lemon in a small mixing bowl. Pour mixture over lamb, rubbing it in well.

3. Place lamb in a pot with a lid; cover and roast in oven for about 2 hours or until very tender.

4. Allow lamb to cool slightly, and then shred with your fingers. Reserve.

5. In a large bowl, toss sweet potatoes with 1 T. olive oil and salt and pepper to taste. Spread potatoes out on a baking sheet and place in oven. Roast until slightly crispy and potatoes are tender, about 15–20 minutes. Remove and let cool.

6. In a sauté pan, heat 1 tsp. olive oil over medium heat. Add spinach and sauté lightly, until wilted. Season with salt and pepper. Remove spinach from pan and reserve to cool.

7. Wipe out sauté pan and place back on stove. Whisk eggs together in a large bowl and stir in 2 tsp. chopped parsley. Season with salt and pepper.

8. Over medium heat, heat 1 tsp. olive oil and add egg mixture. Continue to cook over medium heat until eggs have seized up slightly but are still fairly runny.

9. Arrange four 4-inch metal ring molds on a baking sheet and spray them with pan spray.

10. Place an even layer of cooked sweet potatoes at the bottom of each mold. Add a layer of cooked spinach, then pulled lamb, and then par-cooked eggs.

11. Place baking sheet in the oven and cook until eggs have set, about 10 minutes.

12. In the meantime, place 1 c. feta cheese, 4 tsp. parsley leaves, and yogurt into a blender along with some salt and pepper. Puree until smooth and adjust for seasoning.

13. When frittatas are done, allow them to rest for at least 5 minutes before placing them onto plates and removing ring molds. Sprinkle with remaining crumbled feta and serve hot with yogurt sauce.

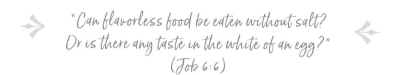

"Can flavorless food be eaten without salt?
Or is there any taste in the white of an egg?"
(Job 6:6)

Shepherd's Pie with Mutton

Yield: 4 servings

Ingredients:

6 T. butter, divided
2 lbs. ground mutton
1 leek, sliced
2 carrots, diced
2 celery stalks, diced
1 T. tomato paste
1 tsp. dried thyme
3 T. all-purpose flour
2 c. chicken stock or broth
1 T. Worcestershire sauce
1 bay leaf
kosher salt and pepper to taste
5 russet potatoes, peeled and diced
4 egg yolks

Instructions:

1. Preheat oven to 425 degrees F.

2. In a large sauté pan or Dutch oven, heat 2 T. butter over medium-high heat.

3. Add mutton and cook until completely browned. Remove meat from pan and reserve.

4. Add leek, carrots, and celery to pan and cook until softened and translucent.

"These are the animals which you may
eat: the ox, the sheep, the goat..."
(Deuteronomy 14:4)

5. Reduce heat and add tomato paste and thyme to pan and cook until tomato paste becomes a darkened brick-red color, about 2 minutes.

6. Sprinkle flour over vegetables and cook, stirring constantly for about 2 minutes.

7. Add chicken stock to pan in small increments, while stirring to avoid lumps.

8. Return mutton to pan. Add Worcestershire and bay leaf and continue to cook for about 5 more minutes, until liquid is thick and mixture is stew-like. Season to taste with salt and pepper.

9. In a separate pot, place potatoes and cover them with water. Bring to a simmer and continue to cook until potatoes are very soft, about 15 minutes.

10. Once potatoes are cooked, drain them well and allow them to steam-dry on the countertop for a couple of minutes.

11. Using a whisk, combine potatoes, egg yolks, and remaining butter; add salt and pepper to taste.

12. Remove bay leaf from mutton. In a large casserole dish, spread mutton filling over the bottom to make about a 1-inch layer. Place potato mixture into a piping bag and pipe it over meat in dollops. Alternatively, spoon potato mixture over top and spread it out evenly using a rubber spatula.

13. Place into oven and cook until potatoes puff up and take on a golden brown color.

14. Allow pie to rest for 10 minutes before serving.

Lamb Manti
with Curried Yogurt and Carrot Puree

Yield: 4 servings

Ingredients:

Dough
1½ c. all-purpose flour
1 large egg
¼ c. warm water
½ tsp. kosher salt

Filling
1 lb. ground lamb
1 yellow onion, minced
1 tsp. ras el hanout spice
1 tsp. kosher salt

Curried Yogurt
1 c. Greek yogurt
1 tsp. garlic powder
2 tsp. madras curry powder
1 tsp. kosher salt

Carrot Puree
3 medium carrots
½ c. chicken or vegetable broth
1 tsp. dried coriander seed
kosher salt and pepper to taste

Instructions:

1. In a stand mixer with a dough hook, combine all dough ingredients and mix on low speed until a smooth dough forms. Remove dough from mixer, cover with plastic wrap, and allow it to rest for at least 20 minutes.

2. In same mixer with paddle attachment, combine all filling ingredients and mix until meat is tacky. Refrigerate.

3. In a small bowl, whisk together yogurt and spices, and place in refrigerator.

4. Peel carrots and cut into 1-inch chunks. Add to a medium pot with a pinch of salt and cover with water. Bring to a boil over medium heat and cook until tender, about 5 minutes, then strain.

5. Add cooked carrots, broth, and coriander to a blender or food processor. Puree until smooth. Season to taste.

6. Preheat oven to 350 degrees F.

7. Flour the work surface and dough as necessary. Using a pasta roller or rolling pin, roll out dough to about 1/8-inch thickness. Cut into 2-inch squares.

8. Add about a tablespoon of meat filling to the center of each square.

9. Using your fingertips, moisten all four edges of the dough squares with water and bring the corners up to the center of the dumpling and pinch all edges closed. This should make a neat, 4-sided pyramid shape.

10. Spray a baking sheet with pan spray and place dumplings on sheet, about ½-inch apart.

11. Bake in oven until filling inside registers 165 degrees F using an instant-read thermometer, about 6–8 minutes.

12. Serve hot with yogurt and carrot puree.

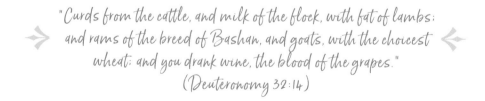

"Curds from the cattle, and milk of the flock, with fat of lambs;
and rams of the breed of Bashan, and goats, with the choicest
wheat; and you drank wine, the blood of the grapes."
(Deuteronomy 32:14)

"Go your way, eat the fat, drink the sweet, and send portions to those
for whom nothing is prepared; for this day is holy to our Lord.
Do not sorrow, for the joy of the Lord is your strength."
(Nehemiah 8:10)

Braised Goat Shoulder
with Carrots and Chickpeas

Yield: 4 servings

Ingredients:

2 lbs. boneless goat shoulder
2 T. olive oil
kosher salt and black pepper to taste
2 oz. all-purpose flour
1 medium yellow onion, diced
4 medium carrots, peeled and cut into chunks
3 T. tomato paste
15 oz. canned whole peeled tomatoes
3 c. chicken broth
4 sprigs fresh thyme
1 bay leaf
1 c. canned chickpeas, drained and rinsed
2 sprigs fresh mint, sliced thin

Instructions:

1. Preheat oven to 325 degrees F.

2. In a large pot or Dutch oven with a lid, add oil and heat over medium-high heat on the stovetop until hot.

3. Season goat shoulder with salt and pepper then coat with flour.

4. In hot oil, sear meat on all sides until deeply browned.

5. Remove goat from pot and reduce heat to low.

6. Add onion to pot and cook gently until tender, about 3 minutes. Stir occasionally.

7. Add carrots to pot and cook briefly, about 1 minute.

8. Add tomato paste and whole tomatoes to pot and cook until slightly thickened, about 5 minutes.

9. Return goat shoulder to pot and add chicken broth, thyme sprigs, and bay leaf.

10. Season liquid with another pinch of salt and cover with lid.

11. Put pot into oven and cook for about 2 hours or until goat shoulder is fork tender.

12. Remove meat from liquid and place in a pan, covered, in a warm area.

13. Skim fat from top of liquid. Add chickpeas and simmer in liquid on stovetop until cooking liquid thickens enough to coat the back of a spoon.

14. Re-season liquid to taste and add meat back to liquid with chickpeas and thickened sauce.

15. Sprinkle mint leaves over braised goat and serve hot.

A very lean red meat animal, goat is a staple protein for peoples all over the world. Many people are tentative about eating goats due to their preconceptions about gaminess or cleanliness, but goat meat can be quite mild and delicate in flavor and is a very sustainable source of meat.

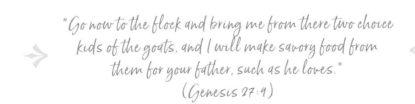

"Go now to the flock and bring me from there two choice kids of the goats, and I will make savory food from them for your father, such as he loves."
(Genesis 27:9)

Grilled Venison Tenderloin
with Olive Relish

Yield: 4 servings

Ingredients:

Venison

2 venison tenderloins (1–1.5 lb. total)
1 tsp. garlic powder
1 tsp. onion powder
kosher salt and pepper to taste
¼ c. olive oil

Olive Relish

3 oz. marinated artichoke hearts
1 c. Spanish or Kalamata olives, pitted
2 scallions, sliced thin
¼ c. parsley leaves, chopped
2 tsp. fresh lemon juice
2 T. olive oil
1 tsp. lemon zest, finely grated
kosher salt and pepper to taste

Instructions:

1. Preheat grill until very hot.

2. Combine garlic and onion powders and sprinkle evenly over venison tenderloins.

3. Season tenderloins generously with salt and pepper.

4. Brush olive oil onto tenderloins.

5. Lay tenderloins onto hot zone of the grill. When sufficient grill marks are achieved, rotate tenderloins to grill other side. When deep, dark grill marks are achieved and internal temp is at least 125 degrees F, remove tenderloins from the grill and allow to rest at least 5 minutes until ready to serve.

6. While tenderloins are resting, roughly chop the artichoke hearts and olives. In a large mixing bowl, combine artichokes, olives, scallions, parsley, lemon juice, olive oil, and lemon zest.

7. Season to taste with salt and pepper. Serve relish with sliced venison.

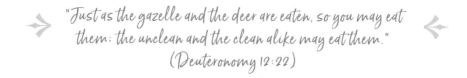

"Just as the gazelle and the deer are eaten, so you may eat them; the unclean and the clean alike may eat them."
(Deuteronomy 12:22)

Lentil Stew

Yield: 4 servings

Ingredients:

1 T. vegetable oil
½ c. yellow onions, diced
¼ c. carrots, diced
¼ c. celery, diced
1 c. red lentils, rinsed and drained
1 tsp. ground cumin
1 tsp. sumac spice (optional)
1 bay leaf
4 c. vegetable or chicken broth
kosher salt and pepper to taste

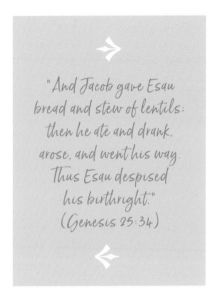

"And Jacob gave Esau bread and stew of lentils: then he ate and drank, arose, and went his way. Thus Esau despised his birthright."
(Genesis 25:34)

Instructions:

1. In a saucepan, heat oil over medium heat until shimmering.

2. Add onions, carrots, and celery to pan. Cook over medium heat until vegetables are tender, about 3 minutes.

3. Add lentils to pan and cook briefly until hot.

4. Add cumin and sumac and cook until aromatic, about 2 minutes.

5. Add broth and bay leaf and bring to a simmer. Simmer until lentils are very tender to the taste and have absorbed most of the liquid.

6. Season with salt and pepper. Remove bay leaf.

7. Serve with matzo crackers or unleavened flatbread (such as *Einkorn Flatbread*, recipe on page 60). Your brother may be willing to offer his birthright for this stew, but let him enjoy a free bowl (plus seconds).

Fresh Pasta
with Dill, Tomatoes, and Mustard

Yield: 4 servings

Ingredients:

Pasta

½ lb. all-purpose flour
2 eggs
1 T. water
1 oz. kosher salt for cooking

Sauce

1 c. chicken broth
2 T. whole grain mustard
1 c. heavy whipping cream
2 oz. unsalted butter
1 T. fresh dill, chopped
4 oz. cherry or grape tomatoes, cut in half
kosher salt and pepper to taste
1 lemon, zested

Instructions:

1. In a mixing bowl, add flour and create a small crater in the center of the mound.

2. Crack eggs into the center of the flour crater. Add water to eggs.

3. Using a fork, beat eggs and water. Continue beating, while rotating bowl and gradually incorporating flour into the egg-and-water mixture.

4. When all flour has been incorporated, dump mixture onto a cutting board or clean surface.

5. Knead dough until smooth, about 3–5 minutes. You should have a firm, elastic dough. If necessary, adjust consistency with more water or more flour.

6. Cover the pasta dough with plastic wrap and allow to rest at room temperature for at least 30 minutes. Then, using a pasta roller/cutter, roll it out to about

¹⁄₁₆ of an inch thickness and cut it into fettuccine or spaghetti. Dust with flour and set aside.

7. In a large pot, add a gallon of water and 1 oz. of kosher salt. Heat to a boil.

8. In a large sauté pan, add chicken broth and bring to a simmer. Simmer broth until it has reduced by ¾. Add mustard and heavy whipping cream and continue to simmer until sauce has thickened slightly.

9. Drop pasta into boiling water along with the butter. Cook for about 2–3 minutes then, using tongs, remove pasta from water and immediately place in sauce with some residual pasta water. Bring pasta and sauce to a simmer and cook until thickened slightly again.

10. Toss pasta with fresh dill and tomatoes and season with salt and pepper. Place pasta in bowls and top with lemon zest.

 "Woe to you, scribes and Pharisees, hypocrites! For you tithe mint and dill and cumin, and have neglected the weightier matters of the law: justice and mercy and faithfulness. These you ought to have done, without neglecting the others."
(Matthew 23:23, ESV)

Sides & Sweets

Millet Risotto
with Fresh Peas and Mint

Yield: 4 servings

Ingredients:

4 c. vegetable or chicken broth
2 tsp. olive oil
½ yellow onion, finely chopped
1 c. millet
¼ c. white wine
½ c. peas, frozen
2 T. unsalted butter
¼ c. plain yogurt
10 fresh mint leaves, chiffonade cut
kosher salt and pepper to taste

Instructions:

1. In a small saucepan, heat broth to a simmer.

2. In a deep skillet or medium saucepan, heat olive oil over medium heat until shimmering.

3. Add onions to pan. Cook over medium heat until onions are tender, about 2 minutes.

4. Add millet to pan and cook briefly until toasty and it begins to crackle and pop.

5. Add white wine to pan and cook, stirring until it is absorbed by the millet.

6. Add hot broth to millet in 1 cup increments, stirring as it cooks. Add additional cups of broth to the millet after each has been absorbed by the grain. Taste for doneness after about 3 cups of broth.

7. When the millet is cooked, add peas to pan and bring back to a simmer briefly.

8. Remove pan from heat and stir in butter, yogurt, and mint leaves.

9. Season with salt and pepper, and serve.

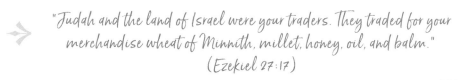

"Judah and the land of Israel were your traders. They traded for your merchandise wheat of Minnith, millet, honey, oil, and balm."
(Ezekiel 27:17)

Ezekiel's Grain Salad

Yield: 6 servings

Ingredients:

2 T. kosher salt, divided
½ c. hard winter wheatberries
½ c. pearled farro
½ c. green lentils
1 c. fava beans, shelled
½ c. pearled barley
½ c. millet
¼ c. olive oil
1 T. fresh lemon juice
10 leaves fresh mint, chopped
kosher salt and pepper to taste

Instructions:

1. In a medium saucepan, bring 4 c. water to a boil.

2. Add 1 T. salt, and the wheatberries, farro, and lentils. Turn down heat to a simmer until grains are tender, stirring occasionally. Remove from heat and strain into a mesh strainer or colander. Spread grains out onto a sheet pan or cookie sheet to cool.

3. Using the same saucepan, bring 4 c. water to a boil.

4. Add 1 T. salt and fava beans and cook to al dente. Remove beans and reserve at room temperature.

5. Add barley to the pan and simmer until just al dente, then add millet. Once millet is tender, strain barley and millet and spread out onto a sheet pan or cookie sheet to cool.

6. Once all grains and legumes have cooled to room temperature, combine in a mixing bowl and add olive oil, lemon juice, chopped mint, and salt and pepper to taste. Toss well to combine.

7. May be served at room temperature or cold.

"Also take for yourself wheat, barley, beans, lentils, millet, and spelt; put them into one vessel, and make bread of them for yourself."
(Ezekiel 4:9)

Kuku Sabzi
(Persian Herb Pie)

Yield: 4 servings

Ingredients:

4 c. scallions, sliced
¾ c. fresh coriander, chopped
½ c. fresh dill, chopped
6 large eggs
2 T. Greek yogurt, strained
1 T. all-purpose flour
½ tsp. baking powder

½ tsp. ras el hanout (Moroccan spice blend)
½ tsp. turmeric
kosher salt to taste
½ c. pine nuts, toasted
2 T. dried cranberries
3 T. olive oil, divided

Instructions:

1. Preheat oven to 350 degrees F.
2. Combine scallions, coriander, and dill in a small mixing bowl. Set aside.
3. In another mixing bowl, combine eggs, yogurt, flour, baking powder, ras el hanout, turmeric, and salt to taste. Stir until smooth.
4. Add the herbs, pine nuts, and cranberries to yogurt/egg/spice mixture. Mix with spatula or wooden spoon until herbs, nuts, and cranberries are coated well.
5. In a 10-inch non-stick sauté pan, add 2 T. of olive oil and heat over medium heat until hot. Add mixture to the pan and with a spatula spread it evenly across the bottom of the pan.
6. Reduce heat to medium-low and cook for about 3–5 minutes. Transfer pan to oven and cook until top of the pie has set and is slightly firm to the touch, about 20 minutes.
7. Remove from oven and allow pie to rest in the pan for about 5 minutes.
8. Invert pie onto a cutting board and cut into wedges. Drizzle with remaining olive oil and serve hot.

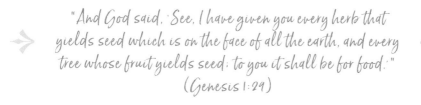

"And God said, 'See, I have given you every herb that
yields seed which is on the face of all the earth, and every
tree whose fruit yields seed; to you it shall be for food.'"
(Genesis 1:29)

Fattoush Salad with Acorn Squash

Yield: 4 servings

Ingredients:

1 acorn squash, peeled, seeded, diced
6 T. olive oil, divided
kosher salt and black pepper
2 pita bread, cut into rectangles
½ fresh lemon, juiced
1 tsp. sumac spice
1 tsp. pomegranate molasses
1 head Romaine lettuce, cut into squares
½ bunch parsley, flat-leaf, chopped roughly
¼ c. mint leaves, chopped roughly
2 Roma tomatoes, diced
1 green bell pepper, diced
1 cucumbers, seeded and diced
1 red onion, sliced thin
3 radishes, sliced thin

Instructions:

1. Preheat oven to 375 degrees F.

2. In a large mixing bowl, toss squash with 1 T. of oil and season with salt and pepper.

3. Spread squash onto a baking sheet lined with silicone or parchment paper. Roast in oven until tender and slightly browned, about 15–20 minutes. Remove from oven and set aside to cool.

4. In the same mixing bowl, toss pita rectangles with 1 T. of olive oil and salt and pepper. Spread out onto another baking sheet and toast in oven, turning every 5 minutes, until browned and crispy. Set aside to cool.

5. In a small bowl, combine lemon juice, sumac, and pomegranate molasses. Whisk in remaining olive oil and season to taste with salt and pepper.

6. In a large bowl, combine remaining salad ingredients with roasted squash and pita chips and toss with salad dressing. Serve cold.

"So one went out into the field to gather herbs, and found a wild vine, and gathered from it a lapful of wild gourds, and came and sliced them into the pot of stew, though they did not know what they were."
(2 Kings 4:39)

Tabbouleh

Yield: 4 servings

Ingredients:

½ c. bulgur wheat, cracked
1 medium English cucumber
1 Roma tomato, diced
1 tsp. kosher salt
3 bunches Italian (flat-leaf) parsley
¼ c. fresh mint leaves, chopped
1 bunch scallions, sliced, green parts only
¼ c. olive oil
3–4 tsp. fresh lemon juice
1 clove garlic, minced fine

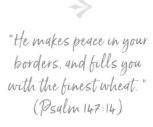

"He makes peace in your borders, and fills you with the finest wheat."
(Psalm 147:14)

Instructions:

1. In a small pan, bring 1 c. water to a boil. Place the bulgur wheat in a mixing bowl and cover with the hot water. Cover with plastic wrap and let soak for about 20 minutes. Taste for doneness; it should be fairly tender when fully cooked. Drain off any excess water and set aside to cool.

2. Cut ends off cucumber and split down the center lengthwise. Split halves down the middle lengthwise to make quarters. Cut the seeds away from the flesh taking care not to cut your hand in the process. Dice the cucumber flesh and combine with tomato in a small mixing bowl; sprinkle with salt and stir to combine.

3. Pick leaves off parsley and chop them coarsely, or tear leaves with your fingers.

4. Add the parsley, mint, and scallions to the cooled bulgur wheat.

5. Drain off excess water from the cucumber/tomato mixture and add it to the bowl with the bulgur wheat.

6. In a separate bowl, whisk together the olive oil, lemon juice, garlic, and salt to taste. Dress salad with mixture, stir, and adjust to taste, adding more lemon or salt as desired.

7. Allow salad to rest for at least 10–15 minutes before serving. Serve at room temperature.

Ful Medames

Yield: 4 servings

Ingredients:

2 c. dried fava beans
kosher salt and black pepper to taste
1 bunch parsley leaves, chopped
1 cucumber, diced
2 eggs, hard-boiled, peeled, and cut in half
olive oil to taste
6 cloves garlic, chopped
1 T. ground cumin
2 fresh lemons, cut into wedges

Instructions:

1. Soak fava beans overnight in a pan of cold water.

2. The next day, drain soaking water and place beans in a pot, covering with fresh cold water. Place lid on pot.

3. Bring water to a simmer and cook until beans are tender, about 2–2½ hours. Season with salt and pepper at the end of the cooking process and remove beans from water, reserving a small amount of liquid.

A very popular Egyptian breakfast dish, Ful Medames can be served as a main dish, a side dish, or a salad. Some fourth-century rabbinic texts mention the making of Ful, and it is well documented that the beans eaten for breakfast were cooked overnight in the remnants of the fires used for heating the public baths.

4. Remove a few beans and mash them into the reserved liquid. Add this puree back into the whole beans to create a sauce.

5. Serve beans with mashed liquid in bowls accompanied with chopped parsley, cucumber, ½ cooked egg, and a splash of olive oil.

6. Garlic, cumin, and lemon wedges can be served on the side as seasoning condiments.

"[They] brought beds and basins, earthen vessels and wheat, barley and flour, parched grain and beans, lentils and parched seeds."
(2 Samuel 17:28)

Einkorn Flatbread

Yield: 6 servings

Ingredients:

12 oz. einkorn flour
1 pinch kosher salt
1¼ c. boiling water
2 T. olive oil
¼ c. butter, melted
extra flour for dusting

Instructions:

1. Combine flour and salt in a large mixing bowl.

2. Add boiling water all at once and stir until combined into dough.

3. Rub olive oil over the dough and cover with plastic wrap; allow to rest for 30 minutes.

4. Heat a cast iron pan or griddle until hot.

5. Dust a cutting board and rolling pin with flour.

6. Cut dough into six equal pieces and roll one into a ball with your palms.

Einkorn translated from German means "one grain." It is one of the oldest strains of wheat grown and consumed by people, notably from the Mediterranean and Middle East, and has a deeper, nutty taste. It was quite likely that Jacob and Esau ate food that was made with einkorn grains.

7. Using the rolling pin, roll out dough into a flat disc about ⅛-inch to ¼-inch thick.

8. Place flatbread onto hot pan or griddle and cook until browned well on both sides and cooked through, about 1–2 minutes per side.

9. Using a spatula, remove the flatbread and brush melted butter on both sides.

10. Repeat using remaining dough balls.

11. Serve warm with *Lentil Stew* (recipe on page 43).

"Take one young bull and two rams without blemish, and unleavened bread, unleavened cakes mixed with oil, and unleavened wafers anointed with oil (you shall make them of wheat flour)."
(Exodus 29:1,2)

Cinnamon Raisin Loaf

Yield: 4 servings

Ingredients:

2 c. golden raisins
1 tsp. vanilla extract
1 c. water
$1/8$ c. unsalted butter, room temperature
1 c. light brown sugar
2 eggs, large
2 c. all-purpose flour
¼ tsp. kosher salt
1 tsp. baking soda
½ tsp. baking powder
1½ tsp. ground cinnamon
½ tsp. ground nutmeg

Instructions:

1. Preheat oven to 350 degrees F.

2. In a small saucepan, add raisins, vanilla extract, and cover with 1 c. water. Bring to a low simmer and simmer for 3 minutes. Set aside to cool.

3. In the bowl of a stand mixer, combine butter and sugar. Using the paddle attachment, cream butter and sugar together until smooth, about 3 minutes.

4. Turn mixer to low and add eggs, one at a time, and incorporate until fully smooth.

5. In a separate bowl, combine flour, salt, baking soda, baking powder, and ground spices.

6. Add cooled water and raisins to mixer, stir briefly, and add in dry ingredients all at once. Stir on low until just combined.

7. Coat a 9×5-inch loaf pan with pan spray and pour in batter. Tap a couple of times on counter to level off batter.

8. Bake in oven until a toothpick inserted in the center comes out clean, about 45–50 minutes.

9. Loaf may be finished with a dusting of confectioner's sugar or eaten as is.

"Then he distributed to everyone of Israel, both man and woman, to everyone a loaf of bread, a piece of meat, and a cake of raisins."
(1 Chronicles 16:3)

Bread Pudding with Figs

Yield: 4 servings

Ingredients:

12 oz. unsalted butter
9 eggs, large
2½ loaves crusty French baguette
6 dried figs, cut into quarters
6 c. heavy whipping cream
1 vanilla bean
3 c. sugar, divided
1 pinch kosher salt
1 T. ground cinnamon, divided

Instructions:

1. Cut butter into pea-sized cubes. Take eggs out of refrigerator and allow butter and eggs to come to room temperature, about 45 minutes.

2. Slice baguettes into ½-inch slices. Lay some in a single layer in a baking pan, closely packed. Insert a third of the fig quarters into spaces between bread slices. Repeat, creating two more layers.

3. In a large pot, combine heavy cream, vanilla bean (seeds and pod), and 1½ c. sugar. Heat slowly over medium heat for about 3 minutes, or until mixture reaches 110 degrees F. Turn off heat.

4. With an electric mixer, cream butter and remaining sugar in a large bowl until very smooth, about 5 minutes.

"And they gave him a piece of a cake of figs and two clusters of raisins. So when he had eaten, his strength came back to him; for he had eaten no bread nor drunk water for three days and three nights."

(1 Samuel 30:12)

5. Crack eggs into a separate bowl. With mixer on medium, add eggs one at a time, allowing each to fully emulsify before adding the next. Scrape down bowl and run mixer for another 15 seconds.

6. Remove vanilla pods from cream. While running mixer on medium (use a whisk attachment if you have one), slowly and steadily add the warm cream until fully incorporated. Add a pinch of salt, 1½ tsp. cinnamon, and mix to combine.

7. Pour custard over layered bread slices until all slices are covered. Dust top of pudding with remaining cinnamon and allow custard to soak into bread for at least 45 minutes, preferably 2 hours.

8. Preheat oven to 350 degrees F.

9. Fill a large pot with water and bring to a boil. When custard has fully soaked into bread, cover with foil and place pan into a slightly larger pan. Carefully fill the larger pan halfway with boiling water.

10. Bake for 1 hour. Remove foil and bake for 30 minutes more, until brown and bubbly.

Ricotta, Almond, and Pomegranate Parfait

Yield: 4 servings

Ingredients:

1 c. fresh raspberries
¼ c. + 1 T. granulated sugar, divided
1 T. pomegranate juice
1 lb. sheep's milk ricotta
½ c. heavy whipping cream
1 tsp. vanilla extract
1 c. Muesli cereal
½ c. almonds, sliced
2 T. unsalted butter, melted

Instructions:

1. Preheat oven to 350 degrees F.

2. In a small bowl, toss raspberries in 1 T. sugar and pomegranate juice. Let stand for about 45 minutes until juices have been released from berries.

3. In a large bowl or stand mixer, beat ricotta, heavy whipping cream, ¼ c. sugar, and vanilla extract until blended well.

4. Combine muesli, almonds, and melted butter in another bowl and mix well. Spread mixture out onto a baking pan and place in oven. Toast for about 8 minutes or until a light golden brown color has been achieved. Allow to cool to room temperature.

5. Spoon 2 T. of cereal mixture into each parfait glass. Follow with a layer of 2 T. of ricotta mixture and then 2 T. of berries. Repeat layers until glasses are filled. Finish parfait by drizzling raspberry juices over top.

"Did you not pour me out like milk, and curdle me like cheese?"
(Job 10:10)

➤ Spiced Nuts and Dates ⬅

Yield: 6 servings

Ingredients:

1 c. raw almonds
1 c. raw pistachios
8 oz. dried dates, pitted and sliced
3 T. olive oil
1 tsp. kosher salt, divided
2 tsp. smoked paprika
1 tsp. dried oregano
1 tsp. sumac spice
1 tsp. dried thyme
1 T. honey

Instructions:

1. Preheat oven to 350 degrees F.

2. Line a baking sheet with parchment paper.

3. In a mixing bowl, toss almonds, pistachios, and dates with the olive oil and half of the salt.

4. Spread on baking sheet and roast in oven for 8–10 minutes, until aromatic and lightly browned.

5. Remove from oven. Return nuts and dates to the bowl, and toss in spices and remaining salt.

6. Spread back onto baking sheet and return to oven for 5 minutes.

7. Remove from oven and drizzle honey over nuts and dates, stir well, and return to oven to roast for 3 more minutes until lightly caramelized. Remove from oven and allow to cool to room temperature.

8. Separate mix, then serve or transfer to an airtight container to store.

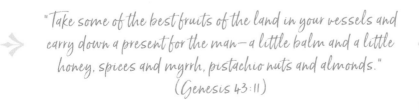

"Take some of the best fruits of the land in your vessels and carry down a present for the man—a little balm and a little honey, spices and myrrh, pistachio nuts and almonds."
(Genesis 43:11)

"For we brought nothing into this world, and it is certain we can carry nothing out. And having food and clothing, with these we shall be content."
(1 Timothy 6:7,8)

FOUR OUNCES PURE HONEY

Spicy Locusts and Wild Honey

Yield: 4 servings

Ingredients:

½ lb. grasshoppers (chapulines naturales)
½ c. vegetable oil
2 garlic cloves, crushed
1 jalapeno, seeded and chopped
½ yellow onion, chopped
kosher salt to taste
1 lemon or lime, juiced
2 T. wild honey

Instructions:

1. In a sauté pan, add the vegetable oil, garlic, jalapeno, and onion. Heat over medium heat until small bubbles form around solid ingredients. Remove from heat and allow warm oil to steep for at least 10 minutes.

2. In the meantime, remove legs and wings from grasshoppers.

Grasshoppers and locusts are very similar in appearance, prevalence, and edibility. Eaten in many cultures around the world, these insects are a very well-known delicacy in Mexico where they are known as "chapulines." The grasshopper is dried, fried, seasoned, and used as an ingredient in dishes, or consumed as a crunchy snack. John the Baptist was known to have eaten this nutritious, delicious, protein rich insect with sweet, fragrant honey.

3. Using a strainer, strain the oil into a small saucepot; discard the garlic, onions, and peppers. Heat oil to 350 degrees F.

4. Fry grasshoppers in oil until golden brown and crispy and drain on paper towels. Season to taste with salt.

5. In a separate bowl, add the lemon or lime juice and combine well with honey. Drizzle over grasshoppers and serve at once.

"Now John himself was clothed in camel's hair, with a leather belt around his waist; and his food was locusts and wild honey."
(Matthew 3:4)

The Hawaiian Table

Chicken Long Rice

Yield: 10 servings

Ingredients:

2 T. of vegetable oil
1 lb. chicken thighs, boneless and skinless
kosher salt and black pepper to taste
1 small piece ginger, peeled and minced
1 onion, sliced thin
4 Shiitake mushrooms, sliced thin
6 oz. cellophane noodles, cut into 3-inch lengths
¼ c. scallions, sliced thin

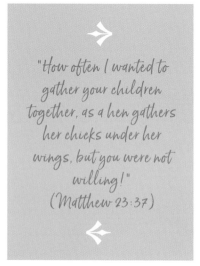

"How often I wanted to gather your children together, as a hen gathers her chicks under her wings, but you were not willing!"
(Matthew 23:37)

Instructions:

1. In a large pot or Dutch oven with a lid, add oil and heat over medium-high heat on the stovetop until hot.

2. Season thighs with salt and pepper and brown both sides of thighs in oil. Sweat ginger and onions in the same pan. Add some of the chicken stock and deglaze the fond.

3. Add remaining chicken stock and bring to a simmer; simmer thighs until they are fork tender, about 25 minutes.

4. Remove chicken meat and shred well. Pour stock through a strainer into a 4-quart pot.

5. Bring stock to simmer again and add mushrooms.

6. Add noodles and simmer, stirring occasionally until noodles are soft.

7. Turn off heat and let noodles rest for about 10 minutes.

8. Stir in shredded chicken and scallions; season to taste with salt and pepper.

Pork, Black Cod, and Taro Laulau

Yield: 4 portions

Ingredients:

1 lb. pork belly, skin removed
1 lb. black cod, boneless, skin on
1 lb. taro root, washed and peeled
15 lbs. collard greens, leaves only
coarse sea salt
4 banana leaves

Instructions:

1. Rinse banana leaves well. Using scissors, cut leaves in half.

2. Dice pork, fish, and taro into 1-inch cubes.

3. Stack 2 leaves of collard greens together. Place 2 cubes of each item onto the leaves, season them with sea salt, and roll them up in the leaves tightly.

4. Arrange the two halves of each banana leaf to form a cross. Place one laulau in the center of each. Bring the leaves up to make a bundle and tie the top with butcher's twine.

5. Place in a steamer basket and steam for 2 hours until the pork is very tender. Serve hot as an entire bundle.

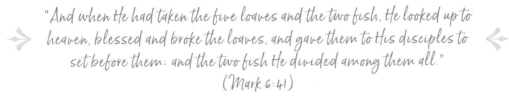

"And when He had taken the five loaves and the two fish, He looked up to heaven, blessed and broke the loaves, and gave them to His disciples to set before them; and the two fish He divided among them all."
(Mark 6:41)

Oven-Roasted Kalua Pork

Pictured with Kalua Pork are Chicken Long Rice (recipe page 76) and poi, which is mashed fermented taro.

Yield: 10 servings

Ingredients:

5 lbs. bone-in pork butt or shoulder
2 banana leaves
½ c. water
1 T. liquid smoke
coarse sea salt
black pepper
2 T. scallions, thinly sliced

Instructions:

1. Preheat oven to 300 degrees F.

2. Using a sharp knife, cut ½-inch slits into the surface of the pork.

3. Season pork liberally with salt and pepper.

4. Wrap pork in banana leaves and place in the bottom of a large pot.

5. Add water and liquid smoke. Cover pot tightly and roast in oven until pork is very tender, about 6–8 hours.

6. Remove pork from pot and remove banana leaves.

7. Pull bone out of pork, shred pork, and season to taste. Top with scallions and serve hot with *Chicken Long Rice* (see recipe on page 76) and poi (mashed, fermented taro).

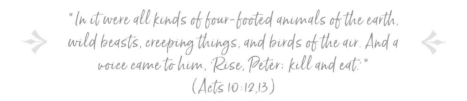

"In it were all kinds of four-footed animals of the earth, wild beasts, creeping things, and birds of the air. And a voice came to him, Rise, Peter; kill and eat."
(Acts 10:12,13)

→ Ahi Poke ←

Ahi Poke (left) with Lomi Lomi Salmon (recipe page 82)

Yield: 4 servings

Ingredients:

1 lb. ahi tuna #1, skin and bloodline removed
½ sweet onion, minced
2 scallions, minced
4 oz. dried nori (seaweed), cut into very thin strips
Hawaiian Alaea salt, or coarse sea salt to taste
crushed red pepper to taste
sesame oil to taste

Instructions:

1. Cut ahi tuna into small strips then into ½-inch cubes and place in a mixing bowl.

2. Combine with onion, scallions, and nori.

3. Add salt, red pepper, and sesame oil and stir well to combine.

4. Place in the refrigerator and allow to marinate for 30 minutes before serving chilled.

> "Poke" is pronounced poh-keh. Poke means to "cut" in Hawaiian. Originally a descriptor of the raw fish that ancient Hawaiian fishermen would eat with sea salt on the way back to shore after a catch, poke is a popular side dish delicacy in Hawaii today. Today's poke can be made with any number of pelagic or reef fish, even octopus. It is also made with countless variations in marinade, such as sesame oil, soy sauce, chili pepper flakes, wasabi, etc.

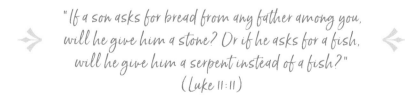

"If a son asks for bread from any father among you, will he give him a stone? Or if he asks for a fish, will he give him a serpent instead of a fish?"
(Luke 11:11)

Lomi Lomi Salmon

Yield: 4 servings

Ingredients:

1 lb. fresh salmon fillet
2 T. coarse sea salt
4 scallions, sliced thin
1 white onion, diced small
4 Roma tomatoes, seeded and diced

Instructions:

1. Rub salt over both sides of salmon fillet. Wrap in plastic wrap and allow to cure in the refrigerator overnight.

2. The next day, wash salt off the exterior of salmon, and dice salmon into ¼-inch cubes.

3. Combine with remaining ingredients and mix well.

4. Allow to marinate in the refrigerator for 1 hour before serving.

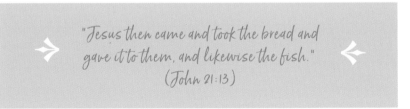

"Jesus then came and took the bread and gave it to them, and likewise the fish."
(John 21:13)

Spam Musubi

Yield: 10 servings

Ingredients:

2 cans Spam
¼ c. soy sauce
¼ c. water
¼ c. sugar
3 c. sushi rice
2 T. canola oil
2 sheets nori (dried seaweed)

Instructions:

1. Cut Spam loaves into slices about ¼-inch thick.

2. Combine soy sauce, water, and sugar in a bowl. Reserve.

3. Wash rice and cook in a rice cooker or in a pot with 3 c. water. Allow to cool.

4. Heat oil in a large sauté pan and add Spam slices. Cook until lightly brown on both sides.

5. When Spam is browned, add soy sauce mixture to the pan and simmer until Spam is coated lightly.

6. Remove Spam from pan and allow to cool.

7. Spread cooked rice evenly onto bottom of a 9×13-inch casserole pan, about ¾-inch thick. Place plastic wrap directly on the rice and press down gently.

8. Place Spam over rice in one even layer, each slice tightly up against the next.

9. Cut between Spam slices and gently lift each musubi out of the pan.

10. Cut nori into 2½-inch by ½-inch strips. Wrap a band of nori around each musubi and serve.

Haupia
(Hawaiian Coconut Pudding)

Yield: 10 servings

Ingredients:

2 c. whole milk, divided
6 T. cornstarch
2 c. canned coconut milk
2 tsp. vanilla extract
1½ c. granulated sugar
1 pinch kosher salt
toasted coconut or cocoa powder

Instructions:

1. Line a 9×13-inch casserole dish with plastic wrap.

2. Place ½ c. of milk and cornstarch in a small bowl and mix until smooth.

3. Combine coconut milk, vanilla, sugar, and remaining milk in a medium pan. Bring to a simmer over medium heat.

4. Once mixture is simmering, gradually whisk in the cornstarch slurry.

5. Continue cooking over medium-low heat for about 10 minutes. Take care not to let the mixture stick to the bottom and scorch.

6. Pour into prepared casserole dish and shake gently to settle mixture. Allow to cool on counter, then place plastic wrap directly on the haupia. Cover tightly and allow to set in refrigerator until firm, at least 3 hours.

7. Turn out of casserole dish onto a cutting board and cut out using a round cookie cutter (or cut into squares).

8. Sprinkle with toasted coconut or dust with cocoa powder.

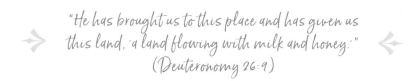

"He has brought us to this place and has given us this land, 'a land flowing with milk and honey:'"
(Deuteronomy 26:9)